A CLOSER WALK

An in-depth Study of God's word for
Young People

OLUKEMI AKINRINOLA, MD

First Edition

ISBN-13: 978-0-9994012-4-8

Visit us at www.olukemiakinrinola.com
www.thelighthousepress.com
Printed in the USA

DEDICATION

I dedicate this book to Men and Women of God,rightly dividing the
Word of Truth,especially to Bishop Israel Ade Ajala, my father in the
Lord, who is an epitome of a great teacher of the Word. He
continues to teach me through word and deed,the privilege of
knowing and serving God.

TABLE OF CONTENTS

God Created The Earth

[Genesis: 1: 1-31]

Memory Verse: "All things are made by him"

(JOHN 1: 3).

∾

God Lives always

Before the Earth was made, before there was a man on this land, God lived. God is everlasting, and He started creation. He has the power to do everything. God created the earth by the Power of His word. The Bible made us know that the Holy spirit was there with him and Jesus was there with Him at Creation. He used the word 'Us' when He started the creation of the world in vs 26.

God made light

At one time there was darkness in the world, and God said, "Let there be light," and there was light. God calls light "Day" and darkness "Night."

God created the heavens

On the next day, a beautiful sky was made by God and the clouds that brought water to grow flowers, trees, and plants, and provided food for men and animals.

God made the earth and the water

There was gathering of water by God into deep and wide sea and land was placed in its right position. A command was made to the sea that they could go so far and not more than their boundaries. Then cover the ground with the light green color of grass and flowers. God gives the man the best place to live, but sin has brought the curse.

God made the lights

There were some light given by God to the earth, but on the fourth day, a command was made by God for creation of light. He made the sun to shine by the day and the moon and the stars by night.

God Put Living Things in the World

After God had created the light to shine upon the earth and had provided a place for man, He put fishes in the seas and birds in the heavens.

God Made Man in His Own Image

God created a beautiful world, and then He put a good man in it. God looked at His world and said that it was "good." He made man out of the dust of the earth and breathed life into him. The mountains and oceans and flowers and everything that God made show how beautiful He is, but only people can love.

Questions:

1. In whose image did God make man? Genesis:1:27.

2. What did God make for man to eat? Genesis:1:29.

3. How do we know that everything was made by God? Colossians:1:16.

4. Was God satisfied with what He had made? Genesis:1:31.

5. How do we know that what we learn from the Bible is true? Mark 13

The Woman Who Disobeyed God

[Genesis19:1-29].

Memory Verse: "Love not the world, neither the things that are in the world"

(I JOHN 2:15).

⌒

The Wicked Cities

Abraham's nephew, Lot, had chosen the land he was living in because it was the right place for his cattle. Abraham had given him his choice. But while the ground he wanted was good for his animals, evil people were living in it. God saw all their wickedness. God hates sin. When men sin they disobey God, and hurt themselves; and God must punish them to help them and to warn others.

God chose to destroy the evil and all the people in them. But Abraham asked God if He was going to kill the right people too when He destroyed the bad. He asked God if He would save the city if there were 50 saved people there. The Lord said He would. Then Abraham asked if He would keep it for 45; the Lord said He would. Then he asked about sparing it for 40 righteous; then for 30; then for 20. The Lord said He would not destroy the city if there were 20 saved ones. Then Abraham asked the Lord not to be offended with him if he asked Him to keep the city for ten. The Lord said He would spare it for only ten. But there were not even ten saved people there.

The Strange Visitors

One evening Lot was sitting in the gate of Sodom. He saw two angels coming near him, and he arose to meet them. He bowed very respectfully to them. Then he invited them to go into his house and stay there all night. He gave them food to eat and treated them very kindly.

The Angels Tell Lot to Leave the City

The angels ask Lot to take his entire family out of the city. It was so wicked God had sent them to destroy it. The angels even took hold of Lot's hand to hurry him out of the town. He told Lot and his family to run to the mountains. When they were out of the city, the fire fell, and Abraham saw the wicked city burning.

Lot's Wife Disobeyed God

The angels had told them not to look back. But Lot's wife must have left something back there she loved, or she was curious to see whether the city was burning, and she looked back. She was punished for her disobedience to God. She became a pillar of salt. Those who obeyed God were saved.

God does not ask us to do anything that is not for our good. He knows what is best for us. Adam and Eve were disobedient in the Garden of Eden, and their disobedience to God and His commandments brought sin and sorrow into the whole world. Jesus was always obedient to God, and God said He was well pleased with Him.

Questions:

1. Why did God send angels to destroy the cities? [Genesis:19:13].

2. Why did God spare Lot and his family? [Genesis:19:16].

3. How did the Lord destroy the cities? [Genesis:19:24-25].

4. What happened to Lot's wife? [Genesis:19:26].

5. What does God say to us about looking back? [Luke:9:62]; [Hebrews:10:38]

The Great Ship

[Genesis6:1-22]; [Genesis7:1-24]

Memory Verse: "He shall give his angels charge over thee, to keep thee"

(LUKE 4:10).

～

The Wicked People

While Adam and Eve disobeyed God, they caused sin and death into the world, and in a short time, the people were so wicked that God decided to send a great flood upon the earth to destroy everything. But there was one man, Noah, who loved God and tried to do the things that pleased God, so God wanted to protect him and his family.

A Great Boat Is Built

God told Noah to make a great ship for him and his family to live in while the water was on the whole earth. He told Noah exactly how to make it and just how big it should be. We believe it was at least 450 feet long, 75 feet broad, and 43 feet high. It may have been even bigger than that.

Noah was told to take into the ark two of each kind of animals and to put food in the ark for his family and the creatures. Of the clean animals, he was told to take seven sets of a kind.

Noah did what God asks him to do. We know it took him 120 years to build that great boat. People would laugh if he made a ship where there was no water, but Noah knew what God had told him and he kept right on building. Noah preached to the people about their sins and about the things that were coming upon the earth and warned them to stop being wicked.

God Told Noah to Go into the Ark

When the ark was ready, God commanded Noah to take his wife, his three sons, and his wives, and to enter the ark. God closed the door. For forty days and nights, the rain fell from the clouds, and the water came from the fountains of the earth and the seas. For 40 days and nights, water filled the earth until everything was covered. Undoubtedly, people rushed towards the hills and mountains, but the water rose higher and higher until the mountains were covered. Then, the ark with Noah and his family floated safely over the highest mountains. We are sure that they thanked God that they were safe, and we are glad we did what God had told them to do.

Questions:

1. Why did God send the flood? [Genesis:6:5-7].

2. Why was Noah spared from the flood? [Genesis:6:8-9]; [2 Peter:2:5].

3. Do you think the door of the ark could have been opened after God shut it? [Revelation:3:7].

4. What did they do for food in the ark? [Genesis:6:21].

5. What happened to all the people and animals outside the ark? [Genesis:7:21].

The Dove And The Water

[Genesis:8:1-22].

Memory Verse: "Prepare ye the way of the Lord"

(LUKE 3:4).

≈

The Great Flood Stopped

God remembered Noah and his family in the ship and stopped the waters from coming upon the earth. He told the wind to blow over the ground and dry it. Gradually the waters began to flow into rivers, lakes, and oceans and the land started to be dry again. When the seas settled, the ship was on the top of the mountains of Ararat.

Noah Sent Out a Raven

Noah opened the window of the ark and sent a raven out, but the raven kept going back and forth as long as there was water over the earth.

Noah Sent Out a Dove

A dove was sent out. To know if the earth had been dry, it would have stayed away, but it came back to the ark. Seven days later Noah sent it out again, and this time it came back with an olive leaf in its mouth. Then Noah waited seven more days and sent it out, but this time it did not come back. Noah knew then that the earth was dry.

More Than a Year in the Ship

Noah and his household and the animals had been on the ship for a long time. But he did not go into the ark until God told him to go, and he did not leave the ark until God told him to do so. Then one day God said that he should bring his family and the animals out of the ark and live again on the earth.

All the wicked people had been drowned. It must have looked very strange to Noah, for the high waters that had washed back and forth had no doubt filled up the low places, and built up high places. It is not easy to find places mentioned in the Bible before the flood because the water must have changed everything very much.

See shells, skeletons of animals, and many curious things are found on the tops of mountains and in the rocks and were no doubt washed there when the waters covered them.

Noah Worships God

The first thing Noah did when he returned to the dry land was to prepare a place where he could worship God. Noah surely thanked God for keeping him safe during that long time when the waters covered the earth and all living things drowned. He must have loved God more than ever before.

God was also pleased with Noah and put a beautiful rainbow in the sky to tell the whole world that he would never again destroy it with a great flood. God always keeps his promise.

Questions:

1. How did the rain finally stop? [Genesis:8:2-3].

2. What kind of bird did Noah send out first? [Genesis:8:7].

3. What did the dove do the first time it was sent out? [Genesis:8:9].

4. Who told Noah to leave the ark? [Genesis:8:15-16].

5. What was the first thing Noah did when he came out of the ark? [Genesis:8:20].

A Kind Uncle

[Genesis13:1-8]; [Genesis14:13-16].

Memory Verse: "Keep yourselves in the love of God"

(JUDE1:21).

∽

God Called a Man He Could Trust

When God wanted a man who would do exactly what He wanted to be done He chose a man named Abraham who lived in a far-eastern country. The people in that country worshiped idols, but we do not know that Abraham ever did. At least, God saw that he would worship the true God when he heard about Him.

Our soldier boys tell us that a soldier is expected to do what his officer tells him to do, and do it when he tells him to do it. God must have seen that Abraham would be that kind of soldier for Him. Abraham believed all that God told him. No doubt that is the reason God blessed him in every way.

Abraham Went Where God Told Him to Go

Abraham must have loved his home and his country very much; but when God told him to leave it, and go to some other place, he did not say he would not go. He obeyed God, and took his nephew, Lot, with him.

Abraham Built an Altar

When Abraham came to a new place, about the first thing he did was to build an altar where he could worship God. Abraham did not forget to love God, to thank Him, and to ask Him to be with him.

Abraham's Servants and Lot's Servants Disagree

Abraham had camels, goats, sheep, and many other animals. Lot did also. But their herdsmen began to quarrel over the pastures for their cattle. Abraham said it was not right to quarrel, and he told Lot that he and Lot must go to different places. He said Lot might choose the land he wanted. Abraham was not selfish. Lot chose the land that had the most water for his cattle, but his choice was not a good one. He chose a place where there were some wicked people. One day wicked kings came and carried him and his family and the cattle away.

When Abraham heard what had happened to his nephew, Lot, he took about 300 of his men and went after the robbers. The robbers were caught and punished, and Lot and his family were brought back.

A king whom Abraham had helped wanted to pay him, but Abraham would not take pay for doing a kind deed.

Questions:

1. Who gave Abraham all that he had? [1 Timothy:6:17]; [Acts:17:28]; [James:1:17].

2. What shows us that Abraham was not selfish? [Genesis:13:9].

3. What does God say to us about being selfish? [Romans:12:10]; [Philippians:2:3-4].

4. Why would Abraham not take a present for being kind to the king? [Genesis:14:23].

5. Does God want us to expect pay for every little act of kindness? [Luke:6:38]; [2 Corinthians:9:7]; [Matthew:10:8].

Abraham Gives Isaac To God

Genesis:22:1-19].

Memory Verse: "Children obey your parents in all things"

(COLOSSIANS 3:20).

❦

God Gave Abraham a Son

Abraham had obeyed God and had gone to the country God wanted him to go to. There God gave him much cattle and silver and gold, and was with him to protect him and help him when he needed God's help.

Abraham had no son, but God wanted him to have a son so that God could make him and his children and their children a great blessing to the world. In one of their families Jesus would someday be born.

God told Abraham that He would give him a son, and Abraham believed that God would do it. He waited 25 years for that son; then a boy whom they named "Isaac" was born. Abraham loved Isaac very much and no doubt thanked God with all his heart for giving him this dear son.

God Asked Abraham to Give Isaac to Him

One day God told Abraham to give Isaac back to Him, the son he loved dearly. It must have been hard for Abraham to be willing to give up his only son, but because it was God Who asked for Isaac, Abraham was willing to give him to God. He knew that God would not ask him to do anything that was wrong. He also believed that God could make Isaac live again if he died.

Abraham Obeyed God

One day Abraham took Isaac to the top of a mountain to give him to God. Isaac, too, seemed to be willing to do just what his father told him to do. But when God saw that Abraham was doing just what He had asked him to do, God told him that he did not need to give Isaac to Him; He would be willing to let Abraham give Him a sheep instead. Then Abraham was glad that he had obeyed God.

God Gives Abraham a Great Reward

God was pleased with Abraham because he loved God well enough to give Him the very best he had and the most beloved. Then

God not only let Abraham have his son Isaac, but gave him much more that was good for Abraham to have. God always gives us much more than we ever could give Him; but we can give Him thanks, and love Him, and do the things that please Him.

Questions:

1. Was Abraham slow to do what God asked? [Genesis:22:3].

2. How could Abraham obey God so willingly? [Hebrews:11:17-19].

3. How did God know that Abraham feared Him? [Genesis:22:12].

4. Did God provide a lamb, as Abraham had promised Isaac He would? [Genesis:22:8], [Genesis:22:13].

5. What was Abraham's reward for obedience? [Genesis:22:16-19].

A Wonderful Dream

[Genesis28:1-22]

Memory Verse: "He will guide you into all truth"

(JOHN 16:13).

∽

Jacob Goes to a Far Country

Jacob had offended his brother, and his mother told him he had better go far away where he would be safe. She told him to go to the home of his uncle. Jacob started on the journey to his uncle's country.

One night when he was about sixty miles away from his home -– sixty miles was a great distance in that day -- he took stones and put them under his head for pillows. He fell asleep and had a wonderful dream. He saw a ladder from earth to Heaven. Angels were going up and down the ladder. It must have been a very beautiful ladder, for above the ladder he saw the Lord standing. The Lord God spoke to him. He said that He was the God of his father and grandfather, and would also be Jacob's God. He told him, too, that the land he was in would belong to him and his children. God said that He would go with Jacob on his journey and would bring him back again in safety.

A Holy Place

When Jacob awoke he marvelled at the beautiful dream he had had. He remembered that He had seen God in his dream and that God had spoken to him, and he said: "Surely the LORD is in this place; and I knew it not" [Genesis:28:16]). And "this is none other but the house of God, and this is the gate of heaven" [Genesis:28:17]).

Then Jacob took the stone and set up a pillar and poured oil on top of it. That was to show that it was holy. He called the place Bethel the house of God.

He Makes a Promise to God

Jacob's heart was grateful to God for what God had shown him and had said to him. He said that if God would be with him and bring him back to his father's home again he would serve God, and he would give God the tenth of what he had. This experience made Jacob a better man than he had been before. God knew just what Jacob would do, and for that reason, no doubt, He gave Jacob this beautiful dream. God knows what we will do long before we ever do it. He knows who will be saved and who will not. He wants everyone to be saved, but not everyone wants to be saved. That is not God's fault; it is their own choice. God wants us to give Him our lives in gratitude for all that He has done for us, and then He blesses us still more.

Questions:

1. What did Jacob say when he awoke? [Genesis:28:16-17].

2. What did Jacob promise God in return for His blessings? [Genesis:28:20-22].

3. Should we pay tithes today? [Malachi:3:8-10]; [Deuteronomy:14:22].

4. How did God punish two people who held back part of the price? [Acts:5:1-10].

5. Does God excuse poor people from paying tithes? [Luke:21:1-4].

A Sermon Jesus Preached

[Matthew5:1-48]; [Matthew:6:9-13]

Memory Verse: "Ye are the light of the world"

(MATTHEW 5:14).

∽

The Sermon from the Mountain

Great crowds followed Jesus from place to place. Some people had heard that He could heal the sick; some had heard that He did very strange things; some had heard that He said very interesting things, and things they liked to hear. And some people were eager to see the Person about Whom they had heard both good things and bad things. Some people believed the untrue things that the people who did not love Jesus said about Him. But He never did anything that was not good.

Perhaps Jesus went up into a mountain so that He could be heard by many people. He also wanted to teach His disciples the things they should know, so that they could teach other people. He sat down and began to talk to them.

Those Whom God Promised to Bless

Among the many things Jesus told the people, He said that God would bless and make happy those who look to Him for help, those who believe God can do anything much better than they can, and that God will show them how to get to Heaven.

He said God would bless the people who try very hard to do what God wants them to do, and to be what God wants them to be. He said that God would bless those who are kind and patient, and help those who need help.

He said God would bless those whose hearts were clean and free from sin.

He said God would bless those who do not cause trouble for people by saying unkind things about them or to them, by saying things that are not true, by being selfish; or in any other way stir up trouble. They will be thoughtful and kind themselves and try to help others to be that way, too.

The Prayer Jesus Taught Men to Pray

The disciples asked Jesus to teach them how to pray, and He gave them the most beautiful prayer, a prayer that has everything in it that men need — the Lord's Prayer [Matthew:6:9-13]).

Questions:

1. How can we be "sunbeams" for Jesus? [Matthew:5:16].

2. What did Jesus say about being angry with our brother? [Matthew:5:22].

3. What should we do if someone strikes us? [Matthew:5:39].

4. How should we treat our enemies? [Matthew:5:44].

5. What did Jesus teach about lending and giving to others? [Luke:6:38]; [Matthew:5:42]; [2 Corinthians:9:7].

Christian Mother

[1 Samuel1:9-28]; [2 Kings4:8-37]; [Luke1:26-33].

Memory Verse: "Children, obey your parents in the Lord"

(EPHESIANS 6:1).

∽

A Christian Mother Is One of God's Great Blessings

One of the greatest blessings a child can have is a Christian mother. She will tell her child about Jesus, about His love, that He died on the Cross to save children from their sins, so that they may go to Heaven to be with Jesus forever. She will teach them to pray and to learn God's Holy Word, and to give their lives to God. The Christian mother can keep her children from doing things that would bring them much suffering, if the children obey what the mother tells them. God has given a commandment with a promise that if we honour our parents it will be well with us and we shall live long on the earth.

A Mother's Prayer Was Answered

A Christian mother, named Hannah, had no son and she wanted one very much. Perhaps she wanted a son so that she could give him to the Lord's work.

One day when she was praying and telling God that if He would give her a son she would give him to God, a good man, named Eli, told her that God was going to answer her prayer. She went away happy, believing that God would keep His promise.

Samuel Was Brought to the Temple

When Samuel, the boy God gave Hannah, was very young, his mother kept her promise to god and brought Samuel to the Temple to serve the Lord. She said she had lent him to the Lord. Hannah probably went often to see her boy and to bring him presents. Samuel became a great and a good man, and was surely thankful to God for a good mother.

Mary Was Chosen to be the Mother of Jesus

The greatest Christian mother was Mary, the mother of Jesus. When God looked down from Heaven and saw many women — some loved God and many did not — He saw one who loved Him very much, and He chose her to be the mother of His Son Jesus.

He sent an angel called Gabriel to tell her that He was going to give her a son whom men would call Jesus. Then angel said He would be a great king, and do wonderful things. Mary believed what the angel told her, and she praised God for choosing her. Perhaps she did not know how very great her Son was to be, but she thought a great deal about what the angel had said to her. Later she saw how wonderful a Son God had given her. God knew she would be a good mother, or He would not have chosen her. Jesus loved His mother, and even while on the Cross, He was thinking of her -- finding her a home and someone to take care of her.

A Good Mother Trusts God

There were many mothers who loved God even before Jesus came to this earth, and God was pleased with them and blessed them. We have read about the good woman who often invited a man of God to come into her home and eat. One day she told her husband that it would be a good thing for them to give him a room in their house, for she believed he was a man of God.

Perhaps he needed to have that room, for he accepted it and no doubt was very thankful for it. One day he called her and told her that God would give her a son.

A Mother Has Faith in the Man of God

One day the boy said he felt sick, and he died in his mother's lap. She laid him on the bed of the man of God, shut the door, and went to look for the man of God. She must have believed that he would pray for the boy and God would raise him up again. When the man of God came to her home, he surely asked God to bring the boy back to life, and God did it.

It is always good to trust God, to believe His Word, and thank Him for all His goodness. It is good, too, to thank God for Christian parents.

Questions:

1. Why is it important for children to go to Sunday School? [Proverbs:22:6].

2. What did Hannah promise God if He would give her a son? [1 Samuel:1:11].

3. Did she keep that promise? [1 Samuel:1:24].

4. Whom should we love even more than our father or mother? [Matthew:10:37].

5. What is promised us if we honour our parents? [Exodus:20:12].

Jesus Heals The Sick

[Matthew:9:18-31]; [Luke:7:12-15];[Mark:2:1-11].

Memory Verse: "I will come and heal him"

(MATTHEW 8:7).

∽

A Little Girl raised from the Dead

As soon as people heard that Jesus could heal the sick, they followed Him wherever He went. The well people brought their sick relatives and friends to Jesus to be healed. We do not read that He ever turned anyone away who came to Him, and He even raised them up from the dead when He saw a funeral.

A little girl, whom a father no doubt loved very dearly, had died. He had heard of the great things Jesus was doing, and he seemed to believe that Jesus could and would raise his child up if He laid His hand on her. Jesus was always glad to help all who came to him for help, and He went to the man's house when he asked Him to come.

The people thought she was dead, but in Jesus' sight she was only sleeping, for Jesus knew that He could awaken her even from death. The people laughed at Jesus when He said she was sleeping. Perhaps Jesus told them to go out of the room because they did not believe He could raise her up again. But all Jesus needed to do was to take her by the hand and raise her up. When the father saw her living again he was surely very glad that he had believed that Jesus could raise her up. It is always a good thing to trust Jesus and to believe His Word.

A Young Man Raised from the Dead

One day when Jesus came into a city He saw a funeral procession. He probably went near to ask who was dead, and He saw a mother walking beside the coffin, crying. Jesus was very kind and He must have felt sorry for the mother when she told Him that it was her only son who was dead. Jesus told her not to cry —— meaning that He would make him live again.

Then Jesus went to the coffin, touched it, and had those who carried it stop; and He said, "Young man, I say unto thee, Arise." The boy sat up and began to speak. How happy that mother must have been when she saw her boy walking around and well again! Jesus was surely always welcome in that home, and the mother and the boy must have loved Him very much.

Many people heard what Jesus had done and they believed that He was very great and very good; and they thanked God that Jesus was there with them.

A Paralyzed Man Healed

One time the people heard that Jesus was in a certain house and they came there with their sick people for Jesus to heal, and to hear Him teach. There must have been a big crowd outside the house; for when the paralyzed man was brought, his friends could not take him through the door because of the crowd. But they were determined to bring him to Jesus, so they took a part of the roof off and let him right down into the room. The roofs of those houses were not made like the roofs of our houses. They were often covered with branches of trees, palm leaves, and some sun-dried mud.

Jesus liked to see their faith and their effort to come to Him for help, and He told the sick man to get up, take up his bed, and go to his own home.

There never was any sickness that Jesus could not heal; and He has just the same power today, and is healing many people who trust Him.

Questions:

1. What should we do when we are sick: [James:5:13-15].

2. What does Jesus expect of us? [Hebrews:11:6].

3. Who heals us? [Exodus:15:26]; [1 Peter:2:24].

4. What question did Jesus ask the blind men? [Matthew:9:23].

5. Did Jesus ever turn a sick person away? [Matthew:12:15]; [Luke:9:11].

Jesus Feeds The People

[John:6:1-13].

Memory Verse: "He hath filled the hungry with good things"

(LUKE 1:53).

～

The People Followed Jesus

When Jesus healed a sick person or raised someone from the dead it was told everywhere; and it made the people want to see Him do those great things, and the sick people wanted Him to heal them; so wherever Jesus went He was sure to have a crowd around Him.

Sometimes Jesus went up into the mountains to rest, but the people would hunt for Him until they found Him, even up there. Sometimes Jesus took His disciples up into the mountains to be alone with them and to teach them many things He wanted them to learn while He was with them, for He knew He would be going back to be with God in Heaven. But the people always seemed to come to the place where Jesus was.

It seemed that people never could forget the kind look on His face and the kind words He spoke. But He also told them when they did wrong things. He would not have been a good friend if He had not.

Jesus Blessed a Small Boy's Lunch

One day when Jesus was up in a mountain talking with His disciples, He saw a great crowd of people there. Perhaps it was a long way that they had come and it would be far for them to go and get food, and the people wanted to stay there and see and hear Jesus.

Jesus asked one of His disciples what could be done to feed all those people, and one of His disciples said it could not be done. Then another of the disciples said that there was a boy who had five barley loaves and two small fishes, but that that would not feed all those people. Jesus knew what He would do, but perhaps He wanted to see what the disciples would do. They would probably have sent the people away hungry, but Jesus was too kind to do that.

He took the bread and the fishes that the small boy had. (We wonder how the little boy felt when his lunch was taken.) Jesus did not forget to thank God for the food. Then He began to give bread and fish to the people, and there was plenty to feed five thousand people. After they had eaten all they wanted, there were twelve baskets full of bread.

Jesus Could Do Everything

Jesus had done a wonderful thing, and only Jesus could have done it. There is nothing that Jesus cannot do; and He can and does just as wonderful things today as He did when He was here on earth. If we obey Him, and trust Him, and love Him, He will do just as great things for us today as He did for the people when He was on earth with them. We cannot see Him, but He is very near to those who love Him.

Questions:

1. What did Jesus do before He fed the people? [John:6:11].

2. What lesson do we learn from this? [Ephesians:5:20]; [1 Thessalonians:5:18].

3. Did the people have enough to eat? [John:6:12].

4. How much was left after they had eaten? [John:6:13].

5. How did the disciples help to feed the people? [John:6:11]

A Baby In A Basket On The River

[Exodus2:1-10].

Memory Verse: "I have chosen you"

(JOHN 15:16).

◠

Joseph's Father Was Called Home to Heaven

After about 17 years of happiness in being near his son Joseph and the other sons, Joseph's father was called to be with God. The brothers were still afraid Joseph would punish them for selling him. They seemed to think that Joseph was waiting until their father died to take revenge on them. But Joseph told them he had no thought of doing such a wrong thing. They had been unkind to him, but he was kind to them. Joseph was too good a man to want to be as unkind to them as they had been to him.

A New King Came

The king to whom Joseph had been brought, and who loved him and gave him a high position, died. A new king came who did not know Joseph and did not care for Joseph's people. The king heard that there were very many of them and he said that he was afraid they might turn against him if there should be a war. He told his men to make them work too hard and it would make them weak, sick, and perhaps cause them to die. He also told them to kill the baby boys, because they might become soldiers and fight against him.

Joseph's People Called on God to Help Them

The people suffered very much because cruel men made them work too hard, and their only hope was that God would somehow help them. God heard their call for help, as He always hears that call. He did not take them out of that place right away, but He was working out a plan that would be a great help to them later.

A Baby Was Placed in a Basket on the River

The cruel king wanted all the boy babies killed, but one mother planned to protect her baby. She prepared a basket that would keep the water out and that would float upon the water. She put it near the edge in the bushes so that it would not go too far out on the river. The baby's sister stood near to see what would happen.

The king's daughter and her friends came to the river to bathe, and they saw the basket on the water. She told someone to bring the basket to her. When she opened it, she saw a beautiful baby and heard the baby cry. That must have touched her heart; and although she saw he was one of the children her father told his men to kill, she did not want this baby killed.

The baby's sister who was watching came near and asked if she should bring a nurse for the baby. The king's daughter said she should get a nurse. The sister went and brought the baby's own mother, but the king's daughter did not know her.

After a few years, the boy was brought to the king's palace to live. The king's daughter, no doubt, loved him very much and called him "Moses," which means, "drawn from the water."

Moses Was Taught the Love of God

We are certain that Moses' mother taught him when he was with her to love God and not to worship the idols the Egyptian people worshipped. God had a great work for Moses to do when he grew older. God knows just what every boy and girl will grow up to be, and He wants them all to work for Him. It is a good thing to begin while young and have many years to work for God.

Questions:

1. How old was Moses when he was placed in the ark? [Exodus:2:2].

2. Who was watching baby Moses from afar? [Exodus:2:4].

3. Who was called to take the baby and care for him? [Exodus:2:8].

4. Do you thing God saw the baby in the basket? [Luke:12:6]; [Psalms:34:15].

5. Why were Moses' parents not afraid to disobey King Pharaoh's orders? [Hebrews:11:23]

The King Grows Weary Of Plagues

[Exodus:11:1-10]; [Exodus:12:1-51].

Memory Verse: "The eyes of the Lord are over the righteous"

(I Peter 3:12).

❧

God Saw the Suffering of the Children of Israel

Joseph's people had suffered a great deal, but God had seen their suffering and had heard their groaning. The King of Egypt wanted to keep them in his country because they worked hard and made bricks for him. At first they were given the straw that was put into the bricks, but now they were forced to find their own straw and make just as many bricks as before. If they did not make a certain number of bricks they were beaten.

God Sent Moses to Help His People

The baby in the basket on the river had become a grown man and had gone away from the king's house. He was far away from there, but

God knew where he was and called him to come to Egypt and help his people.

He gave Moses and his brother Aaron power to do miracles so that the people would know that God was working through those brothers.

God Sent the Terrible Plagues

After the plague of water turning into blood, the plague of frogs, lice, and many other plagues, the king still refused to let them go out of his country.

The King Grew Weary of Plagues

God told Moses to tell the Children of Israel to take the very best lamb of the sheep or the goats, keep it by itself 4 days and then kill it, roast it, and eat it. They were to put some of the blood on the side doorposts of their houses and on the upper doorposts. When He passed through the land that night He would not cause the eldest son to die if He saw the blood on the doorposts. This pointed forward to Jesus.

The Egyptians did not have the blood on their doorposts, and the eldest son in every home died.

Now the king was very glad to let them go out of the country. He must have realized that God was not pleased with the things he was doing.

Moses led the people out of the land as God had told him to do, and they were glad they had obeyed God.

Questions:

1. What was to happen at midnight?
   [Exodus:11:4];[Exodus:11:5].

2. What kind of lamb should they kill? [Exodus:12:5].

3. What should they do with the blood? [Exodus:12:7].

4. Did the Children of Israel obey Moses' commandments?
   [Exodus:12:28].

5. Was the king then willing to let the people go?
   [Exodus:12:31].

A March Through The Sea

[Exodus:14:1-31].

Memory Verse: "Let not your heart be troubled"

(JOHN 14:1).

❧

God Went With the People

When god told the Israelites to go out of Egypt He went right with them to take care of them. In the daytime He led them by a beautiful white cloud, and at night by a pillar of fire. When the cloud stopped, the people stopped. When they followed God they did not go too fast nor go into dangerous places. It is always best to follow God.

The King Tried to Bring Them Back

Although Pharaoh had told the people to go out of his country, he changed his mind and took 600 of his best chariots, and many more chariots, and went after the people of Israel. When they knew that the

Egyptians were following them, the people were afraid. There was a sea in front of them and their enemies were back of them, so they cried to the Lord for help.

Moses trusted God and told them not to be afraid. He said that they should trust God and see what great things God would do for them.

God Told Moses What to Do

God had given Moses power to do great things with his rod, and now God said that Moses should lift up his rod and there would be dry land for his people to pass over. The water would stand like a wall on both sides of the road. Moses obeyed God.

The Egyptians Were Drowned

The cloud with God in it was light to Moses and his people but darkness to the enemies. God let the wheels of their chariots come off and they had much trouble. They wished they could go back, but they could not get out of that place; for Moses again lifted up his rod and the water flowed back into the sea and covered the Egyptians. The people God was protecting walked on dry land and reached the shore in safety. They were thankful to God for His help.

Now they were certain that God was with Moses who trusted and obeyed Him. They found that it was good to do what Moses told them and what God told them to do.

Questions:

1. What sign did the Lord give the people to show them the way? [EXO:13:21-22].

2. What did Moses do that made the waters divide? [EXO:14:21].

3. What happened to the Egyptians in the middle of the sea? [EXO:14:25].

4. Then what did Moses do? [EXO:14:27].

5. Who made the path dry in the midst of the sea? [EXO:14:30].

God Sent Bread Down From Heaven

[Exodus:16:1-36].

Memory Verse: "If ye shall ask any thing in my name, I will do it"

(JOHN 14:14).

～

God Took Good Care of His People

Moses and the people were now very thankful to God for protecting them from the Egyptians, and Moses composed a beautiful song that they sang, praising God for His goodness to them.

They Soon Forgot God's Kindness

The people had been on the way three days and had found no water and were thirsty. They complained to Moses about it. They came to a place where there was water but it was bitter. Then they complained about that. God heard their complaining, and Moses told them that they were finding fault with God and His care over them. But God was still kind to them and told Moses to throw a tree into the water and it would make the water good to drink.

Then they forgot about the water God had given them to drink and began to fear that they would not have food to eat. God heard what they said, but again He was very kind to them. He said that He would rain bread down from Heaven. He would give them meat to eat in the evening (perhaps afternoon) and good bread to eat in the morning.

God Gave the Delicious Manna

God caused a heavy dew to lie on the ground, and on that clean dew, He laid small, white, sweet pieces of manna for them to eat. He said that they should gather only enough for one day. He wanted them to trust Him from day to day; and He would also give them fresh manna each day except the day before their Sabbath. On that day they were to gather enough for two days; so they would not work on their Sabbath. On that day they were to gather enough for two days; so they would not work on their Sabbath, which is our Saturday.

They lived on that wonderful bread from Heaven forty years, and God put so much strength into it they were well and strong and not hungry during the forty years that they were on the way to their new home.

God told them to gather up a small amount of the manna and keep it to tell their children about this bread God had sent them from

Heaven, and to remind them of His goodness and His power to take care of them anywhere.

Questions:

1. Against Whom did the people murmur? [Exodus:16:8].

2. What does the Bible say to us about murmuring? [Philippians:2:14].

3. What kind of food was sent in the evening? [Exodus:16:13].

4. What was sent in the morning? [Exodus:16:14];[Exodus:16:15].

5. How many years did the people eat manna? [Exodus:16:35].

6. Does God ever let people who love Him go hungry? [Psalms:37:25].

The Water That Came From A Rock

[Exodus:17:1-16].

Memory Verse: "If any man thirst, let him come unto me, and drink"

(JOHN 7:37).

～

The People forgot God's goodness to Them

Although God had taken good care of the people with Moses while on their journey through that strange land, they seemed to forget it when they were they were in trouble again. God had gone before them by day in a cloud, and at night in a pillar of fire; and had showed them the best places to travel. When they found bitter water to drink, God told them how to make it sweet. When they needed food, God sent them the delicious manna and quails to eat.

Now they had no water to drink and they and their cattle were thirsty. The seemed to forget that God had given them water before and could do it again. They complained again. It was God they were really complaining against, because God had told them to leave their home in Egypt and go to another country.

When God told them to go through this country He knew that there would not always be water and food for them, but He intended to provide everything for them if they would trust Him to take care of them all the way. They said, "Is the LORD among us, or not?" That was very unkind, and they were very ungrateful to God.

God Had Mercy on Them

When they complained against God and against their leader, Moses, God might have punished them for it and might have permitted them to be without water. But God was kind and merciful again and told Moses what to do to get water for them.

The Water Came from the Rock

Moses had done wonderful things with his rod. Now God was going to give him power to do another miracle. God said that Moses should take three men with him and go to a rock He would show him. God would be there.

God told Moses to strike the rock with his rod. Moses did as God told him and water came out of the rock, and the people had plenty of good water to drink. God always gives the best of everything.

Only God could cause the water to come out of a rock, but there is nothing that God cannot do. They should have trusted God and not have complained. When they complained they complained against God Who had done many wonderful things for them. They should have been thankful to God and should have trusted Him because He had always helped them when they needed Him.

Questions:

1. Why did the people murmur this time? [Exodus:17:3].

2. Was the Lord pleased with their murmurings? [Psalms:78:18-21].

3. What did the Lord tell Moses to do? [Exodus:17:5-6].

4. Who brought the water out of the rock? [Exodus:17:6]; [Psalms:78:16].

5. Who held up Moses' hands? [Exodus:17:12].

Jesus Stills The Tempest On Galilee

[Matthew:8:24-27]; [Matthew:4:18-22]; [Luke:5:1-11].

Memory Verse: "Follow me, and I will make you fishers of men"

(MATTHEW 4:19).

~

Beautiful Galilee

Every Christian loves to think of the Sea of Galilee because Jesus spent so much time there. We can easily picture Him walking on the shore looking at the blue sky and the blue water below the blue hills.

The Fishermen

Jesus watched the fishermen as they drew in their nets with fish for there was much fish in that water. One day when Jesus wanted some money for His disciples He told them to go and catch a fish and they would find money in its mouth [Matthew:17:27]). All the fishes did not have money in their mouths but Jesus knew how to put it there when He wanted to.

There were good fish and bad fish. The good fish the people ate, and the bad fish they threw away. Jesus said that was like people -— the good and the bad people. The good people would be taken to Heaven to be with God forever and always be happy, while the bad people would be sent to a place where they would be punished for the wicked things they had done.

Fishers of Men

One day when Jesus was walking on the shore of the sea, He saw two brothers, Peter and Andrew, fishing. He perhaps saw that they were very good fishermen and He wanted them to be with Him so that He could teach them more important work. He wanted to tell them about Heaven and teach them that they must have their sins forgiven so that they could be with God in Heaven. He also wanted to teach them to tell others how to be saved. He said to them: "Follow me, and I will make you fishers of men."

Then He saw two more brothers, James and John, fishing, and He called to them, too. They all came just as soon as Jesus called them to Him. It must have made Jesus happy to see how quickly they came when He called. Jesus wants all people to come to Him when He calls them.

At another time He was sitting in a ship, teaching the people on the shore. When He had finished, He asked Simon to push the ship out into the deep water and let down the nets. Simon answered that they had fished all night and had caught nothing. However, he obeyed the Lord. Then they caught so many fish in the net that it broke. They had to call to their partners in the other ship to come to help them, and both ships wee filled with fish and began to sink. The reason they caught so many fish was that they had obeyed Jesus.

The Storm Stilled

The Sea of Galilee was about 13 miles long and about 7 miles wide, and great storms came up quickly. One day when He and His disciples were crossing the sea there was a storm. The waves were so big that they covered the ship. Jesus always worked hard, teaching the people and healing the sick, and He was often very tired. He said, too, that the birds had nests and the foxes had holes, but He had no place to lay His head. Being tired, He was asleep in the ship when the disciples came to Him, awoke Him, and said: "Lord, save us: we perish." He asked them why they were afraid; they should have felt safe when He was with them. Then He told the wind to stop blowing, and the waves to be still. And the sea was still. The disciples were very much surprised that the winds and waves obeyed Him.

After they had been with Jesus a while they found He could heal the sick and raise the dead; and that He had power over the wind, the waves, and over everything, and that He was the Son of God.

Questions:

1. What was Jesus doing when the storm arose? [Matthew:8:24].

2. Who calmed the storm? [Matthew:8:26].

3. What did the men say then? [Matthew:8:27].

4. Is there anything that Jesus cannot do? [Matthew:28:18].

5. Did Simon obey Jesus and let down his net? [Luke:5:5].

6. What happened then? [Luke:5:6].

MIRACLES OF JESUS

[John:2:1-16]; [John:4:46-54].

Memory Verse: "Whatsoever he saith unto you, do it"

(JOHN 2:5).

❧

Preparation for Work

Jesus had been preparing to do the work He had come to this world to do. He had been baptized by John, not because He needed to be baptized, but because He did everything that the Word of God told those who loved Him to do. God was pleased with what Jesus was doing, for He spoke out of Heaven and said: "This is my beloved Son, in whom I am well pleased" [Matthew:3:17]).

When the wicked one had tried to get Jesus to do wrong, when He was in a place where there was no food and He had eaten nothing for forty days, Jesus did not obey what the wicked one said. He obeyed only what God said.

A Christian's Joys

Jesus is willing to help us in our sickness and troubles, but He is also with us when we are happy. He wants people to be happy. He came that we might be glad forevermore. People who love Jesus and do what He tells them to do are always happy.

God has given us many things to enjoy. He made the sky a beautiful blue, the clouds soft and white; He gave us green trees, green grass, and lovely flowers of many colours. God has given us the singing of birds, and the sweet sounds of music. All these things were given us for our happiness.

Good Friends

Besides our loving parents and brothers and sisters, God has given us kind friends. We all love to have friends to be with us when we are in trouble, and also when we are happy. We read in the Bible that Jesus had loving friends, too. He had no home of His own, but we read that He sometimes stayed in the home of His friends –– Mary, Martha, and Lazarus. We read, also, that He was invited to people's homes to eat; and, perhaps, He went there knowing that He would have a chance to talk to them about God.

One time He was invited to a wedding in Cana. Cana was not far from His hometown. Perhaps the people in that home where the wedding was were His relatives. Jesus and His mother and His disciples were there.

Before they were through eating and drinking, Jesus' mother came to Him and said that they had no more wine to give the people. We do not believe that the wine they had there was the kind that makes people drunk. Almost everyone likes grape juice. God gave us the grapes with the delicious juice in them, but people sometimes spoil it by letting the juice become sour and so bad that it make people drunk.

Mary told the servants to do just what Jesus said. She seemed to know that Jesus had the power to do anything He wanted to do. When Jesus tells us to do a thing we should do it just as He tells us to do it, and do it as soon as possible. They filled the big jars with water. Then Jesus turned the water into such a sweet drink that a man said they had kept the best wine until last. This was the first thing Jesus did that showed the disciples and His friends that He was very powerful.

Questions:

1. What did the mother of Jesus say to the servants? [John:2:5].

2. Did the servants know who made the water into wine? [John:2:9].

3. Was it good wine that Jesus made? [John:2:10].

4. What did Jesus do to those who were selling things in the Temple? [John:2:15].

5. What is one important thing to remember when we go to church? [Luke:19:46]; [1 Timothy:3:15].

Jesus Talks With A Ruler

[John:3:1-21].

Memory Verse: "Ye must be born again"

(JOHN 3:7).

⌒

The Kingdom of God

Heaven must be a beautiful place. We see many lovely places here on earth, but God has told us in His Word that no eyes have seen such beautiful things as there are in Heaven; no ears have even heard about such great things; and people have not been able to imagine how wonderful Heaven is. Jesus said he was going away to prepare a place for those who love Him, and we know that when Jesus prepares a place, it will be the very best that could possibly be.

We love to be with kind people, so we know it will be the greatest joy to be with Jesus and with God the father, Who are the kindest and best of all who are on earth and in Heaven. And when we go to Heaven we shall be there forever and always be happy. Jesus came to this earth to die for us so that we might be with Him always in His lovely Home.

The Punishment

When Jesus died on the Cross He took upon Himself the punishment that we would have had for the bad things we have done. But because Jesus died for us, we can be forgiven for our sins.

Getting Ready for Heaven

Heaven is a clean place. So the people who live there must be clean and holy. Heaven would not be a safe and beautiful place if people who do bad things were allowed to go there. God could not have wicked people in His Home. So they must be made clean and ready to be there with God.

When Jesus was on earth He taught what they must do to be ready for Heaven.

Born Again

A teacher, one who should have known what to do to be ready, came to Jesus and said he knew that Jesus was also a teacher, Who had come form God, for no one else could do the great things that Jesus did. Then Jesus told the man, Nicodemus, that every man must be saved or he could not go to Heaven. The man did not know what that meant, so perhaps Jesus explained that one must be sorry that one ever did such wrong things as stealing, lying, swearing, getting angry, hating people, and many other bad things. He said that those who did such things must ask God to forgive them; then He washes the heart and makes it white and clean.

Jesus gives one a heart that wants to please Him instead of wanting to disobey Him. When God has made that change in a heart then one is "born again." God wants all men to be saved – to be "born again." And Jesus came to earth to tell people how they could be born again, and He did everything He could to help them to have their sins forgiven and be made ready for their home in Heaven with Jesus.

Questions:

1. What must we do to be ready for Heaven? [John:3:3].

2. Did Nicodemus know how to get saved before Jesus told him? [John:3:9].

3. Does Jesus ever turn a hungry soul away? [Luke:1:53]; [Psalms:107:9].

4. How did Jesus make it possible for us to be saved? [John:3:16].

5. What does "born again" mean? [1 Peter:1:23]; [1 John:5:18].

The Woman At The Well

[John:4:1-42].

Memory Verse: "Let him that is athirst come"

(REVELATION 22:17).

❧

The Well

Perhaps few of us have ever seen the wells they used to have before the pump with the handle came into use, or the faucet we turn on and off today. When we have plenty of water we do not stop to think how good it is to have it. But to the one who is in a country where it is hard to get good, clean water it is very important. We read that Abraham always built an altar and dug a well when he stayed in a place any length of time. Both were very important.

During the war the soldier boys often suffered very much from lack of water, especially if their planes fell where they could not get clean water to drink. Sometimes they wanted water more than they wanted food. Jesus knew how necessary water was.

In some countries they dig wells that sometimes are not very deep, perhaps only 20 or 30 feet deep. There they tie a bucket to the end of a rope and lower the bucket into the well by a handle on which the rope is wound. Then the handle is turned and turned until the rope is wound back on the handle and the bucket full of water is at the top of the well.

Jesus at the Well

One day Jesus was very tired from walking and from talking to people and teaching them. So He stopped to rest at a well. It is thought that this well was one that Jacob had dug many years before. It was about 100 feet deep. It can still be seen today.

While He sat there resting, a woman came with her water pot upon her head and perhaps with her rope to let her bucket or jar down into the water. Jesus asked her to give Him a drink. Then He told her that if He gave her a drink He would give her a drink of water that would keep her from ever being thirsty again. She could not understand what kind of water that could be. She told Him that the well was deep and He had nothing with which to draw the water — no rope and no bucket. She wanted to know how He could give her water to drink. Then He told her about the water He had to give — forgiveness for her sins and power to live right. He called it "living water." He said that if she drank of that water she would never thirst again. Then she knew that He was Jesus. She went to her home and told many people about Him, and they came to see Him and hear Him tell the things they needed to hear.

No doubt, Jesus knew that that woman would come there to get water and He wanted to tell her some things she needed to know. Jesus is always looking for those who want to see Him and want Him to help them. We should thank Him and love Him with all our hearts that He does that. We believe that the woman at the well did love Him for all that He had told her and had done for her.

Questions:

1. Why was Jesus sitting on the well? [John:4:6].

2. What were the first words Jesus said to the woman? [John:4:7].

3. Did the woman at first know who Jesus was? [John:4:10].

4. Of what kind of "water" was Jesus speaking? [Isaiah:12:3]; [Revelation:21:6].

5. What was the testimony of the Samaritan woman after she met Jesus? [John:4:39].

Jesus Can Heal Any Disease

[Matthew:8:1-16].

Memory Verse: "With God all things are possible"

(MARK 10:27).

~

The Many Sick People

It did not take long before the people found out that Jesus could heal them. He made the blind able to see. He healed the lame people so that they could walk. The sick were raised up and made strong well. He even raised up the dead. Those who were well would bring their sick people to Jesus to be healed. Wherever He went many people followed Him. We do not read in the Bible that Jesus ever sent a sick person away without healing him. We are thankful that He has the same power today, and is healing all who put their trust in Him.

Nothing Too Hard for Jesus

Some people think that if it is a very serious disease Jesus cannot heal it; but we read in the Bible that He healed every kind of disease.

He make the body in the first place, and it is very easy for Him to make it well. We know that the man who can make an automobile can surely fix any part that does not work well.

One day a man with a terrible disease called leprosy came to Jesus to be healed. The man probably had great sores on his body, and people were afraid to come near him. But Jesus was not afraid to touch him. When the man worshipped Jesus and said that he knew He could make him well if He wanted to, Jesus said He wanted to make him well. He touched the man's sore body and said, "Be thou clean," and right away the man was made well. We are sure he must have loved Jesus very much for doing that.

A Soldier's Faith

At another time a soldier came to Jesus and told Him that his servant was sick. He must have believed that Jesus was well able to heal his servant, for he said that he himself had many soldiers under him and when he told one of them to go and do something, he would go; when he told another soldier to come to him that person would come. Then he said that if Jesus said the word the sickness would have to leave his servant. Jesus likes to have people believe Him. When He says that He is able and willing to heal people, He likes to have them believe it. Jesus was pleased when He saw that the soldier that his servant would be healed; and he was healed at the very time Jesus said that he would be healed.

Another Healing

Jesus came to Peter's home and there He saw Peter's wife's mother sick with a great fever. Jesus just touched her hand and she was able to get right up and do her work. It was very easy for Jesus to heal her.

A Wonderful Friend

We have many kind friends and we are thankful for them, but in Jesus we have the best friend of all. He not only saves us from our sins, but He gives us the rain and the sunshine that make things grow; and He gives us food and clothing four our bodies. He also heals us when we are sick if we love him, pray to Him, trust Him, and do what He tells us to do.

Questions:

1. Did the leper believe Jesus could heal him? [Matthew:8:2].

2. Did the Centurion feel worthy to have Jesus come to his house? [Matthew:8:8].

3. Why did Jesus marvel at him? [Matthew:8:10].

4. Can we be healed without faith? [James:5:15]; [Mark:9:23].

5. How was Peter's wife's mother healed? [Matthew:8:15].

God Spoke From The Mountain

[Exodus:19:1-25].

Memory Verse: "The Lord is my helper"

(HEBREWS 13:6).

⮂

Our Kind God

Moses and his people had been on the march for about three months and God had taken very good care of them all the time. To guide them and perhaps protect them God gave them a cloud by day. At night He led them with a light. When there was no water He even made it come out of a rock. If the water was not good where they were camping, He told them how to make it good. He gave them manna from Heaven, and they were never hungry. He made their clothes last a long time. He kept them strong and well to travel. But even though God was so very kind to them, they often complained. When they were sorry and asked God to forgive them, God forgave them and went on helping them as a kind father helps his children.

But God is the kindest of all fathers, and we should be thankful to Him and love Him always.

God - The Teacher

The time came when the people should go to God's school and learn what He wanted them to do, and how to worship Him in the right way. God told Moses, and Moses told the people. Moses loved and obeyed God and God often talked to him.

They reached a good place to camp, and here was a mountain that God had chosen to come down upon when He spoke to the people. God called Moses up into the mountain, and told Moses that if the people would obey Him He would give them many good things, and make them happy. When Moses told the people what God had said, they answered: "All that the LORD had spoken we will do." But they soon forgot their promise. Sometimes people make promises to God when they are sick or are in need of God's help; and when God heals them and helps them, they forget the promises they made to Him.

Clean People

God wants people to have clean hearts, and He told Moses to tell the people to make themselves clean for the third day when He would talk to them through Moses.

God said that He would come down to the mountain, but that the people must not try to come up to see Him. They must not even touch the mountain. Not even the cattle were to be permitted to touch the mountain. It had become a marvelous place because God was there. Moses knew what to tell the people to do to make themselves clean.

Our Wonderful God

On the day set by God there was thunder and lightning from the mountain, and the mountain shook. God came down to the top of the mountain. He called Moses up to Him. Moses would never have dared to go up there if God had not told him to come.

God knew what the people would likely do, so He warned them not to come near the mountain; if they touched the mountain they would surely die. God told Moses and Aaron what He wanted them to teach the people; and what they learned then is a help to us today. He taught them to fear God, obey Him, love Him, and trust Him. When they did as God told them to do, they were happy. When we do what God tells us to do, we too are happy and we may look forward to being with God in Heaven forever.

Questions:

1. How did Moses keep the people from getting too near the mountain? [Exodus:19:12].

2. What would have happened if anyone had touched the mountain? [Exodus:19:12].

3. How did the people prepare for the day that the Lord would talk to them? [Exodus:19:14].

4. What happened to the mountain when the Lord came down? [Exodus:19:18].

5. Whom did the Lord call up into the mountain? [Exodus:19:20-24].

The Tables Of Stone

[Exodus:20:1-26].

Memory Verse: "It is I; be not afraid"

(JOHN 6:20).

❧

Our Holy God

When the people saw the lightning, and the smoke, and heard the thunder, they knew that God was on the mountain. Moses told them they did not need to be afraid if they obeyed what God had told them. They were afraid to have God speak to them, so they asked Moses to speak to them.

God's Voice

God spoke from the mountain in a voice that could easily be heard by the people. He told them that He was their Lord God Who had brought them out of Egypt, and had taken such good care of them all the way. He wanted them to know that they could still trust Him and obey Him.

God's Commandments

God told the people some of the things we should do for Him, and some things we should do for others.

He said that we should love God more than anyone else.

- ➢ He said that we must not worship idols.

- ➢ We must not swear.

- ➢ We must keep God's day holy.

- ➢ We must honour and obey our parents.

- ➢ We must not kill anyone.

- ➢ We must not steal

- ➢ We must not lie.

- ➢ We must not want what belongs to others.

The Tables of Stones

God called Moses up to Him in the mountain and gave him the tables of stone upon which He had written the commandments. Moses was up in the mountain forty days, and God told him many things He wanted His people to know and do.

Questions:

1. Who gave Moses the Ten Commandments? [Exodus:20:1].

2. Were the people afraid when God spoke from the mountain? [Exodus:20:18].

3. What did the people say to Moses after God finished speaking? [Exodus:20:19].

4. How does God speak to us today? [Hebrews:1:1-2]; [Psalms:119:105].

5. Commit to memory: [Exodus:20:3] and [Exodus:20:12].

The Tables Of Stone Broken

[Exodus:32:1-35];[Exodus:34:1-7],[Exodus:34:33-35].

Memory Verse: "No man can serve two masters"

(MATTHEW 6:24).

⤳

The Idol

Because Moses stayed so long up in the mountain, talking with God, the people thought he was not coming down again. Then they wanted an idol. They should have known that an idol could not lead them as Moses had led them and that it was wicked to worship an idol instead of God. They seemed to have forgotten how good God had been to them.

Aaron had told them to bring their earrings. Men and women wore them, and they had given them to be made into the idol. They probably had seen an idol like a calf worshipped in Egypt, and they wanted that kind of idol.

A Terrible Deed

God knows just what is going on in the earth, and He saw what the people were doing. He told Moses to go down again, for they were doing a terrible thing. He said He would punish them very much.

Broken Tables

When Moses saw that the people were dancing around the idol, he threw the tables down and they were broken. Then he took the idol and melted it in fire, ground it into powder and made the people drink it in their water. They had done a wicked thing and he had to punish them for turning to an idol and dishonoring God.

The Prayer of Moses

God said they were a very disobedient people and He would not go with them any longer. But Moses begged Him to have mercy on them and go with them as before. Then God forgave them and said He would go with them. God is very kind and merciful, and forgives when men are sorry for their sins and ask God to forgive them.

New Tables of Stone

God told Moses to make two new tables of stone and bring them up to Him in the mountain, and He would write on them what He had written on the first ones.

God's Great Glory and Brightness

God told Moses that he could not see God's face or he would surely die. He said no one could look at His face and live. He told Moses that He would pass by him but God would put His hand over Moses' face and Moses would see only His back.

Moses Obeys God

Moses did what God told him to do. God passed by Moses and said He was the One Who was kind, merciful, and good. We know He is just the same today. How thankful we should be that we have such a loving God and Father, and such a loving Friend as Jesus!

Questions:

1. What did Aaron make for the people to worship? [Exodus:32:4].
2. Did the Lord see it? [Exodus:32:7].

3. What did He say to Moses? [Exodus:32:7-10].

4. What did Moses do when he saw the calf? [Exodus:32:19-20].

5. Why did Moses cover his face with a veil? [Exodus:34:33-35].

A Beautiful Tent

[Exodus:35:1-35]; [Exodus:40:33-38].

Memory Verse: "In my Father's house are many mansions"

(JOHN 14:2).

~

God's Glory

Because Moses had been near to God, his face shone so brightly that he had to cover his face when he talked to the people. He had much to tell them of the things God had said to him. God had told him what he should do to help them keep true to Him, and then God would go before them and protect them against their enemies.

The Tent-Church

The people were not to stay in Sinai a long time but were to go on to the land into which God was leading them. So God told Moses to have the people make a tent-church in which to worship Him. This church could easily be carried with them on their journey.

Willing Workers

Moses asked the people to give what they could to make the tent and the things in it. He said that those who had a willing heart should bring an offering to the house of God. God wants only the things we give to Him willingly. The people seemed to be glad to do it. Some brought gold, wood, spices, skins, and anointing oil. Those who could weave, made cloth and curtains for the tent. For every part of the work that needed to be done there was someone who knew how to do it. No doubt, God had taught them and prepared them for it.

The blue, and scarlet, and purple curtains must have made the tent very beautiful.

The tent was carried by certain men whom Moses appointed. And they carried it just as God had told them.

The Altars

There were altars upon which the offerings were laid that were brought for the worship of God. God has given us much, and He expects us to give Him something in return, especially our love.

The Appointed Workers

God told Moses to choose certain ones for every kind of work to be done. And some of them had to be dressed in a special kind of clothing. God told Moses just how it should be, and Moses did what God told him. God was pleased with the way they had obeyed Him. God told them He would tell them when to set up the Tabernacle and begin the worship.

God's Blessing

When the Tabernacle, or tent-church, was finished, God covered it with a cloud in which He was present. Moses could not even go into it because of God's presence there.

When they journeyed on, there was a cloud over the tent by day, and a bright light at night so that all the people could see it. This made them know that God was there with them, leading them. God plans everything well. If we do just what God tells us to do and when He tells us to do it, we shall always be happy and it will please our heavenly Father.

Questions:

1. What kind of offering did the Children of Israel bring unto the Lord? [Exodus:35:29]

2. What kind of offerings should we bring to the Lord? [2 Corinthians:9:6-7].

3. How should we act when we come into the house of the Lord? [1 Timothy:3:15]; [Psalms:100:4].

4. What happened when Moses had finished the work? [Exodus:40:34].

5. How did the Children of Israel know when to travel? [Exodus:40:36-37]

A Brother And Sister Murmur

[Numbers:12:1-16]

Memory Verse: "Do all things without murmurings"

(PHILIPPIANS 2:14).

~

Moses' Brother and Sister

We remember the story of the baby Moses who was hidden in the little ark by the river's bring. His sister, who stood afar off to watch, no doubt was Miriam about whom we are now studying. Moses also had a brother, named Aaron.

Moses had been called of God to be the leader of the Children of Israel. Aaron and Miriam had been very helpful to Moses many times. We know that God loved Aaron, for at the time that God came down upon the mountain He called Moses and Aaron up into the mountain so that He could talk to them. However, sometimes Aaron and Miriam did things that displeased God very much and must have made Moses feel very bad.

We remember how displeased Moses was at the time that he came down out of the mountain and found that his brother Aaron had sinned and made golden calf for the people to worship. They should have kept right on worshipping the true God, even though their leader Moses was up in the mountain for a time. These people knew that Moses had prayed for them many times, and God had answered his prayers.

Brothers and sisters can be a great deal of help to one another if they love one another and love Jesus. But if they are not saved and quarrel and are unkind to one another, they can bring much trouble and sorrow into their lives.

God Hears Murmurings

The Lord had told the people at one time that when they murmured, it was not against Moses and Aaron, but against God. Just so it was now. Aaron and Miriam murmured against their brother Moses — so they thought. But it was really against God, and He heard it, too.

When a child murmurs against a minister of the Gospel or even against his Sunday School teacher, it actually is against God. We should be careful always to obey those who are trying to teach us how to follow the Lord. A child is also murmuring against God when he murmurs against his parents. God said, "Do all things without murmurings and disputings" [Philippians:2:14]). Sometimes a parent will tell a child to do something and the child will ask, "Why?" We should go at once and do what we are told to do by our parents, without having to know the reason: "Children, obey your parents in all things."

The Punishment

We read that a terrible thing happened to Aaron and Miriam as punishment for their sin. The Lord came down in a cloud and stood in the door of the Tabernacle and called Aaron and Miriam. He rebuked them for the wrong they had done; He also asked them if they were not afraid to speak against Moses. Then Miriam became a leper.

Leprosy is a very bad sickness, and in many instances in the Bible the Lord punished people with leprosy when they sinned. The skin becomes white, and sometimes there are sports or sores all over the body. However, the stains of sin on a heart are even worse than the sports of leprosy on the skin. It takes the Blood of Jesus to heal the leper and it also takes the Blood of Jesus to save the sinner.

Moses prayed for Miriam to be healed; but she had to be shut out of the camp for seven days. Then she was brought back into the camp and the people could go on their journey. This was a good lesson for

Miriam and Aaron as well as for all the people in the camp. It is also a good lesson for us to remember. God does not like murmuring.

Questions:

1. Why was it wrong for Aaron and Miriam to murmur against Moses? [Numbers:12:6-8]; [Hebrews:13:17].

2. How was Miriam punished for murmuring? [Numbers:12:10].

3. Who prayed for Miriam to be healed? [Numbers:12:13].

4. How long was she shut out form the camp? [Numbers:12:15].

5. Is Jesus displeased when we murmur? [Philippians:2:14].

6. When we murmur, against whom is it? [Exodus:16:8].

The Land Of Milk And Honey

[Numbers:13:1-33]; [Numbers:14:1-45].

Memory Verse: "I go to prepare a place for you"

(JOHN 14:2).

~

Nearing the Homeland

When the people led by Moses were nearing the land to which they were going, the Lord told Moses to send 12 men to go to see what the land was like; to see whether the people were strong or weak, and whether they lived in tents or in strong buildings. By seeing the land and the people, they would know how to take the land; for God had told them that He was going to give it to them.

The Bad Report

After 40 days they came back and told Moses and the people that the land was very good, there was much food there; and they brought back a bunch of grapes that took two men to carry. They said that the people were big and strong, and the spies looked like grasshoppers beside them. They said, too, that the cities had very high walls around them.

When the people heard that report, they were afraid. They said they could not take that land and those people, and blamed Moses for bringing them up to that place where they would have to go in and fight.

The Good Report

But there were two men who believed God, trusted in His power and were willing to go in and take the land. Caleb and Joshua knew that if God had told them He would give them that land, He would help them to get it. They knew that there was nothing impossible with God.

The Punishment

Because the people did not believe God's Word and trust Him to do what He had said He would do, God was not pleased with them; and He punished them for their disobedience. Instead of going into that good land they had to turn back into the wilderness and suffer hardships for forty years. Many of the people who had come out of Egypt never did get into that good land. Only the children twenty years old or under twenty were permitted to go into the land many years later.

God punished the spies who brought back an evil report – the Lord sent a sickness on them, and they died. But Caleb and Joshua were not punished.

It is a terrible thing to disobey God, and not to trust Him. When God tells us to do a thing, He will always help us to do it, no matter how hard it may seem to be.

Questions:

1. What kinds of fruit did the spies bring back? Number:13:23.

2. What did Caleb and Joshua say about the land? [Numbers:13:30]; [Numbers:14:7-9].

3. What did the other spies say? [Numbers:13:31-33].

4. What happened to those who brought back an evil report? [Numbers:14:36-37].

5. Were Caleb and Joshua also punished? [Numbers:14:38].

The Animal That Talked

[Numbers:22:1-41]; [Numbers:23:1-30].

Memory Verse: "The Lord hath sent his angel"

(Acts 12:11).

⤳

Fear in the Nations

The nations that did not worship the true God had heard about the way God had been helping the Children of Israel conquer nation after nation, and there was great fear. Some of the kings were friendly and permitted the people to go through their country, but some were not friendly and went out to fight them and stop them. God remembered those who were kind to His people, and rewarded them; and He remembered those who were not kind and He punished them.

King Balak

A king called Balak feared that his country would be taken by the Israelites. He knew a man who seemed to believe in the God of Israel and he sent for that man.

Balak told Balaam to curse those people -– ask God to harm them so he could defeat them. He told Balaam that he could give him much money and honor for it.

Balaam wanted to do it to earn the money. But God told him he should not curse His people. Balaam told Balak he could not do it, but Balak kept on insisting. All the while Balaam wanted to do it, and God knew he wanted to, so God let him go, to try to curse them.

The Donkey and the Angel

God always tries to keep us from doing anything that is wrong for us to do, but we do not always listen to Him and obey him. He set an angel with a drawn sword in Balaam's path. The donkey saw the angel but Balaam did not. The donkey turned aside and Balaam beat him. Then the donkey went against the wall and Balaam's foot was crushed by the wall. Then Balaam beat the donkey again. Now the donkey fell down, and again Balaam beat him.

Then the Lord gave the donkey power to speak, and it asked Balaam why he was beating it. Balaam said he would even kill it if he had a sword. He was very angry.

God let Balaam's eyes be opened to see the angel and the sword. God told Balaam that the donkey had saved his life by turning away from the angel that would have killed Balaam if he had gone on.

Sin in His Heart

Balaam at last knew that God was using the donkey to keep him from doing that wrong thing. Then God made Balaam bless the people instead of curse them, and Balak knew that God was helping the Children of Israel. But Balaam was finally killed in a battle. His heart was not right with God, for in his heart he was more eager to get the money, even if it were by doing wrong, than he was eager to please God.

Sometimes children beg to do things after their parents have told them "no". God knew what was right, and when He said "no" it was what was best. Balaam should not have wanted to do what God told him not to do.

Questions:

1. Was God pleased that Balaam went with the princes of Moab? [Numbers:22:22].

2. Why did Balaam want to go? [Numbers:22:17].

3. How did Balaam treat his donkey when it turned aside? [Numbers:22:23].

4. What did Balaam do when he finally saw the angel? [Numbers:22:31].

5. What happens if we insist on having our own way? [Proverbs:14:12].

The Man At The Pool Of Bethesda

[John:5:1-16]

Memory Verse: "The Lord shall raise him up"

(JAMES 5:15).

His Healing Power

How glad we should be that Jesus can and is willing to heal all our sicknesses. It does not matter what kind of sickness it is, for there is nothing too hard for Jesus to do. The man who can make an automobile or any other thing can easily make right any part that gets out of order. God Who made our bodies in the first place can easily heal any part of us that gets out of order. We are happy to read in the Bible that God is willing to do it, for He has told us in His Word that if people will pray and believe God He will heal them.

We call for the ministers to pray for us, and we pray, because the Bible tells us to do that. We have seen many times that God heals the sick when they believe His Word and trust Him. It is a wonderful thing to have a Friend like Jesus!

The Sick Man at the Pool

There was a pool, or pond, that people were eager to get into after the angel had stirred it up at certain times. Jesus came by that pool one day and saw a sick man lying near the pool. He had been sick 38 years. Jesus always felt sorry for anyone in trouble and he asked the man if he would like to be healed. The man did not know he was talking to One Who could do all things, and he said that there was no one to help him into the pool after the angel had trouble it. He said others always went ahead of him.

It was not necessary for the man to be carried to the pool this time, for all Jesus needed to do was to say, "Rise, take up thy bed, and walk." Jesus gave the man the strength he needed to get right up and walk. That is the way Jesus does; when He tells us to do something, He is willing to give us the help we need for what He tells us to do.

The man was made well right away. He took up his bed and walked away from that place where he had been so many times in the 38 years. How thankful he must have been to Jesus for making him well again!

Men Who Did Not Love Jesus

There were some people who did not love Jesus because He told them they were wicked. Jesus told them they were doing things that were wrong and He wanted to help them to be good, but they did not want to do good. They said that it was Jesus Who was doing things that were not right, but that was not the truth. They watched Jesus to see if they could find some fault in Him, but Jesus never did anything but what was good.

The men who did not love Jesus said that He should not heal the sick man and that he should not carry his bed on their Sabbath day. But he told them that Jesus said he could do it. We must obey God rather than obey men.

Then they wanted to know who it was that had told him to take up his bed and walk. The man said he did not know who He was. Jesus had gone away, but He found the man He had healed and told him not to sin any more or something worse might come to him.

Telling Others

As soon as the man who was healed heard that it was Jesus Who had made him well, he told other people about Him. He was so glad that he was well that he wanted everybody to know about the One Who could heal them.

We are glad that somebody told us about Jesus and His power to save us from all our sins and to heal us when we are sick. We want to be faithful and tell others about Him. It is sad that there are so many people who do not seem to know about Jesus and His love.

Questions:

1. What did Jesus say to the man at the pool of Bethesda? [John:5:8].

2. Did the sick man obey the command? [John:5:9].

3. Did he know Who Jesus was? [John:5:13].

4. What did Jesus do for this man when He found him in the Temple? [John:5:14].

5. What is more important to us, healing or salvation? [Mark:8:36-37]; [Matthew:6:33].

A Beautiful Home

[John:14:1-14].

Memory Verse: "I am the way, the truth, and the life"

(JOHN 14:6).

⁓

Away from Home

Jesus had left His beautiful home in Heaven where He had lived with His loving Father. He came down to this wicked earth and lived more than 33 years. He had no home here. He was hated by some of the wicked people because He told them that they were wicked and could not go to Heaven unless they stopped doing what was bad. They did not like to hear that, so they planned to kill Him.

But Jesus knew how wicked the people were and how much they needed Him to help them to be better. He came to be crucified so that all people could have their sins forgiven and go to be in Heaven with the Father and with Him. It made Him sad to see the wickedness of the world. We read that He wept, but we do not read that He laughed. He knew that He had a hard trial before Him -- the Cross.

Going Home

When Jesus talked to His disciples about leaving them, it made them sad because they did not quite know that He meant that He was going back to be with God in Heaven. So He tried to tell them about that place He was going to prepare for them, too, if they believed what He told them and obeyed what He said.

He said, too, that He would come back for them and take them with Him to that wonderful place, to be with Him always.

The Heavenly City

If Jesus prepares the place, we know it will be a beautiful one. He knows how to do all things. He has the power to do everything. He owns everything. He can create anything. We know He loves beautiful things, because He has given us so many lovely things — the blue sky, the white clouds, the sun, the bright moon and stars, the lakes, the green trees, the birds, and the many kinds of flowers. If the flowers and trees are beautiful here, how much more beautiful will the flowers of Heaven be! We read in the Word of God about the trees with twelve kinds of fruit. It also tells us about the river with the green trees on its banks. The Bible tells us about a lovely rainbow round about the throne of god.

Sometimes before God calls people to come to be with Him He lets them see a little of Heaven. Some people have seen the streets of gold; some have seen flowers; some have seen the angels; some have seen happy people. Some have seen the bright light -– Jesus is the light there. Some have heard the sweet music.

Heavenly Music

We have heard sweet music here on earth, but it is not so sweet as the music will be in Heaven when the angels sing, and the people whom God has saved sing around the throne of God, thanking Him for His love and for their happiness in being up there with Him.

We read in the Bible about those who play golden harps. And we believe there will be many kinds of musical instruments played in Heaven by those who will play them beautifully. God has told us in His Word that ears have not heard such sweet sounds as there will be in Heaven. We cannot even imagine how beautiful it will be.

But if we are going to sing God's praises in Heaven we must begin here on earth. We must be made ready here to sing the heavenly songs up there.

No Sorrow There

We read in God's Word that no one is sad in Heaven; no one cries; no one is ever sick; no one dies. It must be a very happy life there not for a few years, but forever.

The Way to that City

There is something we must do, too, to be made ready to live in such a place. Heaven is a clean place, and those who will live there must also be clean in every way. They must have their sins washed away, and be made holy. Jesus gave His life that all who wants to be made good enough to be in Heaven with Him can be.

We should be very thankful to Jesus for what He has done for us; and for the beautiful Home we shall have if we obey Jesus, trust Him, and love Him. Someone has said that those who want to walk on the golden streets of Heaven must be as pure as the gold of those streets. The Word of God tells men how to be made pure. Jesus said, "I am the way, the truth, and the life." We thank Him for showing us the way.

Bringing Others with Us

A person would be very selfish if he did not want to bring others with him to such a wonderful place as Heaven. We need to have Jesus teach us how to get ready, and how to help others to be ready, to go to be with Jesus when He comes for those who love Him. We should be glad that someone told us about Jesus and we should always be faithful in telling others about His love.

A little girl in India learned in the mission school about Jesus and Heaven and God. She learned that it was a wonderful place to which good people went when they died. Her parents lived in a village where they worshipped idols, and did not know about a loving Father in Heaven. When the little girl went to her home in the village, she told her parents about this beautiful place. Her mother said, "Yes, when you die you can go to that lovely place, but when I die I cannot go there. You must stay with me and be where I am." Then the little girl went back to the mission school and asked if some missionary would go to her home and tell her mother about Jesus so she, too, could go to Heaven.

Questions:

1. What is another name for Heaven? [John:14:2].

2. Who may enter Heaven [Psalms:15:2].

3. Why did Jesus come to earth? [John:3:17].

4. Do we know when the Lord is coming to take us to Heaven? [Matthew:24:36].

5. The wicked people cannot go to Heaven. To what place will they be sent? [Psalms:9:17].

Teachings Of Jesus

[Matthew:6:14-34]; [Matthew:7:1-29].

Memory Verse: "Ask, and it shall be given you"

(MATTHEW 7:7).

∾

The Best Teacher

Boys and girls in school have good teachers who want them to learn to read, to write, to count, and how to take care of their bodies and minds. But Jesus wanted to do more than that: He wanted to tell people how to know and love God. He left His beautiful home in Heaven and came down to this earth where He had no home. We read in the Bible: "Foxes have holes, and birds of the air have nests; but the Son of man hath not where to lay his head" [Luke:9:58]). He was away from His Father's Home in Heaven more than 33 years, just to be down here to teach people how to be good, and make it possible for them to be with Him in that wonderful Home someday.

Forgiving

One of the things Jesus taught people was that they must forgive. Sometimes people do things that we do not like; perhaps they say unkind things to us. But Jesus said that we must not angry at them, must not hate them, and must not want to "get even." Sometimes children will say, "He hit me, and so I hit him." That is not what Jesus said we should do. He said that if a person hits us on one cheek we should let him hit the other, too. Many people think that is a hard thing to do; they think they should strike back.

Jesus not only said men should forgive those who were unkind to them, but He did it, too. When they said unkind things to Him, said things about Him that were not true, He did not answer them. When they slapped Him in the face and laughed at Him, He kept still. Even when they hung Him on the Cross to kill Him, He prayed for them and said: "Father, forgive them; for they know not what they do" [Luke:23:34]).

Having Our Sins Forgiven

Before we can ever go to be in Heaven with Jesus we must have our sins forgiven. God is the only One Who can forgive our sins. But Jesus tells us that if we expect to be forgiven we must forgive other people. Jesus taught that, when He taught the disciples that beautiful prayer: "Forgive us our debts, as we forgive our debtors." We must forgive everything and not have a bad feeling in our hearts toward anyone. If we do not forgive others, our heavenly Father cannot forgive us.

When we have done a wrong thing to others we must ask their forgiveness. This is not always an easy thing to do, but it is what Jesus said we should do. We must not only ask to be forgiven, but we must be sorry that we did the wrong thing, and ask God to help us never to do it again. One day a man came to Jesus and asked Him if he forgave his brother seven times would that be enough. But Jesus told the man he must forgive 70 times seven. Some people will not forgive at all. Some think they do well if they forgive once or twice, but Jesus said they must forgive as often as 490 times.

The Test

If we do not like to have our brothers and sisters take or break our things, then we should not take theirs. If we like to have the good things, then we should remember that they like them also. If we expect them to be kind to us, then we must be kind to them. If we want them to help us when we need it, we must help them when they want us to do so. If we do not like to have them be selfish with us, we must not be selfish either. If it makes us happy to have them be fair with us, we must remember that it makes them happy to have us be fair with them. If we want them to love us, we must love them.

We should always remember to give the others the best and take the worst for ourselves. For instance, if you and your friend had two apples, one very nice apple and one poor one, you should take the poor one and give your friend the nice apple. We should always give our brothers and sisters the best.

If all people would remember what Jesus said, and would do it, there would be no quarrelling or fighting or hating. He said: "Therefore all things whatsoever ye would that men should do to you, do ye even so to them: for this is the law and the prophets" [Matthew:7:12]).

Questions:

1. Where should we keep our treasures? [Matthew:6:20].

2. Who feeds the birds? [Matthew:6:26].

3. How does Jesus tell us to treat others? [Matthew:7:12].

4. Do many people find the strait gate and the narrow way? [Matthew:7:14].

5. What happened to the house that was built upon the sand? [Matthew:7:27].

Anointing Of Jesus' Feet

[Luke:7:36-50].

Memory Verse: "Thy sins are forgiven"

(LUKE 7:48).

❧

Not Friends

One wonders how people could be so wicked as not to see that Jesus was their very best Friend. Those who were lame were healed so that they could walk. The blind people had their eyes made well and they could see. The mothers and sisters who wept when their dear ones died were made happy again when Jesus raised them from the dead. We read that He went about doing good everywhere. Many people did love Him.

But there were some people who hated Jesus. They even wanted to kill him. They hated Him because he told them they were not doing what was right. He told them they were wicked and if they did not have their sins forgiven they would not go to Heaven. They did not like to have Him tell them that they were bad people. But Jesus had to tell the truth, and he wanted them to know they were bad, so that they would stop doing bad things. He was willing to help them to be good. He came down to this earth to tell people how they should live so that they could go to be in Heaven with Him forever. But some of the people hated Him for telling them the truth, and planned to put Him to death.

Good Friends

There were men and women who did love Jesus, and who were glad He told them what was wrong and what was right. They wanted to do the good things, and not the bad. They saw all the good things Jesus did, and they loved Him very much. Wherever He went many people followed Him. So many people followed Him and wanted Him to help them that He often became very tired and had to go to the mountains or away by Himself to rest and to talk to God His Father.

He seemed to like to stay in a home with two women called Mary and Martha, and their brother Lazarus. Lazarus was the man who died and Jesus called him right out of his grave. Mary and Martha and Lazarus loved Jesus very much, and we are certain they were happy to have Him in their home, whenever He came. It is wonderful to have a home where Jesus can be also! Children who have Christian fathers and mothers are very fortunate. Many children in the world today never hear their father or mother tell them about Jesus; are not taken to the Sunday School where they may learn more about Jesus. Children who do have fathers and mothers who pray, read the Bible, and worship God, should pray for the children who are not so fortunate, and should thank God for Christian parents.

A Friend's Home

A man invited Jesus to come to his home to eat with him. Jesus was always glad to have a chance to tell people about His Father in Heaven, and about the beautiful home they could have if they would love and obey Jesus.

While Jesus was in this man's home a woman came with a box that had very expensive and sweet oil in it. She knew Jesus would help her in her trouble, and she washed His feet with her tears and wiped them with her long hair. She poured the sweet oil over His feet.

The man of the house thought she was not a good woman and he thought Jesus should send her away. But Jesus wanted to help her to be good. When she asked Jesus to forgive her sins He gladly did it. Jesus is always glad to forgive a man's, a woman's or a child's sins when he is asked to do so.

Questions:

1. What four things was the woman doing for Jesus? [Luke:7:38].

2. What did the Pharisee have to say about that? [Luke:7:39].

3. Did Jesus forgive the woman's sins? [Luke:7:48].

4. Was it through the woman's kindness to Jesus, or her faith, that she was saved? [Luke:7:50].

5. Is it necessary for us to have faith in order to be saved? [Hebrews:11:6].

The Rich Man

[Luke:12:1-34].

Memory Verse: "Be content with such things as ye have"

(HEBREWS 13:5).

∽

Our Needs Supplied

One day as Jesus was preaching to the people the crowd was so great that they were actually stepping on one another. He taught the people many things they should know so that they could go to Heaven someday. One very important point He taught them that day was that people should not try to lay up many riches here on earth. He taught them that making sure of a home in Heaven was much more important than having much money in the bank or owning many fine things.

He talked to them about the birds — they have plenty of food and don't have to work hard for a living. Jesus sees to it that they have plenty to eat. He also told them that the lilies of the field do not have to work — yet they wear the most beautiful clothing. So Jesus told the people not to worry about what they should eat or drink, because He knows our needs, and will give us everything we need if we do what He tells us to do.

The Rich Fool

Jesus told the people a story of a man who became very rich. His crops were so great that he did not have enough room in his barns for all his fruit and goods. He was storing away as much money and goods for old age as he could gather together. One day he decided to pull down his barns and build bigger ones so he would have more room. Then he could "eat, drink, and be merry." He did not think of what God would say about that.

Just then a Voice spoke to him. It was the Voice of God telling him that he was going to die that night and leave all his goods behind. God called him a fool, because he had laid up treasures here on earth but did not have any treasures up in Heaven. No doubt, he had thought only of himself and how much money he could earn. Perhaps he was too busy making money to have time to help the poor people and the suffering ones.

That night when the rich man died, he left all his riches behind -- he could not take even a penny with him. When he was born into this world, his fists were closed tightly; but when the time came for him to leave this world, his hands were wide open.

A Rich Man's Dream

A story is told of a rich man who dreamed that he died and went to Heaven. An angel met him and led him by the hand to show him his home. As they walked along the golden streets they passed by many beautiful homes. Presently he saw a man standing in the doorway of a very lovely home, and recognised him as his former servant. The rich man thought: If my servant has such a lovely home, surely I will have a larger and more beautiful one.

They kept on walking through the beautiful city and the homes were smaller and smaller until there was just a tiny cottage. The angel told the rich man that this was his home. He was very much disappointed when he saw it. But the angel said: "This is all the material you sent up to build it." It taught him a lesson. Of course this was only a dream and no one will be disappointed in Heaven. No one will be jealous. But it is good for us to remember that we must lay up our treasures in Heaven.

Our Treasure

The treasure in Heaven is our love for God, our love for His Holy Word, our love to work for Him our love to be with Him always. We lay up treasure in Heaven when we help others to go there — by bringing children to Sunday School where they may learn about God and about having their sins forgiven. Another way to lay up treasure is to visit the sick people and give them money or food if they need it. Jesus said that if we did kind things to others we were doing them to Him. If we bring many people to Jesus we shall shine "as the stars for ever and ever" [Daniel:12:3]). If we trust Him, have our sins forgiven, Jesus will give us what we need to eat, give us a home, and clothes to wear, and all that we need on earth; but, best of all, He will give us the lovely things He has for us in Heaven.

Questions:

1. What did the rich man decide to do? [Luke:12:18].

2. What did God say to him? [Luke:12:20].

3. Does Jesus want us to worry about food and clothing? [Luke:12:22], [Luke:12:28-29].

4. What does He tell us to seek after? [Luke:12:31].

5. Who will give us everything we need? [Philippians:4:19].

Blessings And Cursings

[Deuteronomy:27:11-14]; [Deuteronomy:28:1-68].

Memory Verse: "Obey them that have the rule over you"

(HEBREWS 13:17).

❧

Good Things Promised

Moses wanted the Children of Israel to have all the good things God could give them. He had promised that they should be the people of God and be very happy. He was going to give them a good home, plenty of food, and everything they needed. If the people would only obey the voice of God and do as He told them, there were many other good things for them: they would be blessed in the city, in the field, or wherever they went -- even everything they owned would be blessed.

So Moses told them that after they had passed over the River Jordan they should get together and talk about the things that would please God and that he would bless; and the things that would displease Him and He would curse. Moses told them that some of them should stand on one mountain and call to the people on the other mountain and tell them that the Lord would bless them if they did what God told them to do. Then all the people should say with a loud voice, "Amen." This means, So be it.

Moses said that the rest of them should stand on another mountain and call to the other people and tell them that the Lord would be displeased and punish them if they disobeyed. And all the people should again say, "Amen." We find that after the death of Moses, Joshua did exactly as Moses had told him to do. Joshua was always obedient to what God told him, and God blessed him for it.

To the Children

The Lord wanted these people to know and understand what He wanted them to do, so they could teach their children. He told the parents to talk to the children about God when they sat in the house, or when they were out walking, or when they were in bed. They were even told to write the words of God upon the posts of their house and upon the gates. God is not pleased with parents who fail to teach their children the Bible lessons.

A Little Girl

Today also, the Lord blesses the people and the children who obey Him but He also punishes those who disobey Him. A little girl was punished for her disobedience. Her mother asked the child's older sister to take a pail of milk to a neighbour. The younger sister insisted she wanted to do it; the mother told her she was too small to go alone. When the little girl insisted, the mother let her go. The child started down the road, but soon returned — crying, covered with milk and dirt. She had fallen down, hurt herself, and spilled the milk. The mother reminded her that it was her punishment for disobedience.

A Disobedient King

We read in the Bible of a man who did not obey God. King Saul was told to go to a certain city and destroy the whole city. He went to that city and destroyed everything except the wicked king and some of the best animals. Afterward, King Saul told the prophet of the Lord, Samuel, that he had done as the Lord commanded him. But Samuel said that he heard the lowing of the oxen and the bleating of sheep. Saul explained it by saying that the people had spared the animals in order to make sacrifices to the Lord. The man of God knew that was not the truth and the real reason. Saul perhaps wanted the best cattle for himself. Samuel told the king that to obey the voice of the Lord was the most important thing of all [1 Samuel:15:22]). He also told Saul that since he had disobeyed the Lord, he could no longer be king. God did not answer his prayers.

A Mother and Son

A faithful mother used to tell how she talked to her children about the Lord. She would talk to them while they were out in the yard, or out walking, or in the house. She wanted her children to know more about the Lord and know what He wanted them to do. Her little boy would come to her and ask permission to do something or go somewhere. She would look in the Bible and find the answer there. If the Bible forbade doing whatever he wanted to do, that would settle it for him.

The Lord saved him and has blessed him all through his life because he obeyed his mother and the things she taught him out of the Bible. He grew up to be a man whom God uses in a wonderful way.

Questions:

1. Name five ways in which the Lord would bless the people if they would obey Him. [Deuteronomy:28:3-14].

2. Name five ways in which He would curse them if they would disobey. [Deuteronomy:28:16-45].

3. What does the Bible say about children obeying their parents? [Ephesians:6:1-3].

4. Did Jesus obey His parents? [Luke:2:51]; [Hebrews:5:8].

5. Upon what conditions does Jesus bless people today? [Matthew:5:3-11].

Moses Goes And Joshua Comes

[Deuteronomy:34:1-12]; [Joshua:1:1-18].

Memory Verse: "Lo, I am with you alway"

(MATTHEW 28:20).

❧

God's Goodness to the People

God had been very patient with the people who complained against Him and against Moses so very often. God had given them water when they needed it, and manna for food. He had taken such good care of them that their clothes and their shoes had not worn out all those years. When they complained and disobeyed and God needed to punish them, Moses would pray for them and ask God to have mercy on them; and God would forgive them. Moses could do that because he loved and obeyed God. God forgave them because He loved Moses.

Near the Promised Land Again

After many years of troubles and discouraging wanderings in the wilderness, they had come back to the place where they were to cross the Jordan River and come into the good land that God had promised to give them.

But God told Moses that because he had made a great mistake when he struck the rock twice to get water when God had said, "Speak ye unto the rock" [Numbers:20:8]), he could not take the people into the good land. God said Moses would die.

Moses Called to Heaven

The people had often complained about the food and the water and the hard travelling, and had caused Moses much sorrow; but the people seemed to love him and he loved them, and had been with them a long time. After he was taken from the little basket on the river he was in the king's house 40 years. Then he was in a lonely place 40 years, taking care of sheep and cattle, when God called him to come and lead the people out of their hard life in Egypt and to the good land he had for them. He had led the people nearly 40 years and was an old man. Even though he had been a good man and had always obeyed God, when he made a sad mistake God had to punish him for it.

God told Moses that He would take him to the top of the mountain and show him the wonderful land to which they had been travelling all those years, but Moses would not be the one to take the people into it. Then Moses died, and the Bible tells us that God buried him. No one has ever found his grave.

Moses was 120 years old when he died. God said that there never was another prophet like Moses whom the Lord knew face to face. God loved Moses because Moses loved God and obeyed Him and with the exception of this one instance was faithful in what God told him to do.

Joshua Chosen

Joshua had been a faithful worker with Moses and now God called him to be the leader of the people. God told Joshua that as he had been with Moses so He would also be with Joshua. This must have been a great encouragement to Joshua, because he knew he had a hard task before him. The people did not always obey God.

God told Joshua to be brave, and he would go with him wherever he went. Then He told Joshua to take the people across the Jordan River into the good new home He had for them.

Obedience Promised

When Joshua told the people what God had said to him, they said that they would do just what Joshua told them to do, and they asked God to bless Joshua as he had blessed Moses. But they sometimes forgot their promises.

Questions:

1. Did Moses get to go over into the Promised Land? [Deuteronomy:34:4].

2. Who buried Moses when he died? [Deuteronomy:34:6].

3. Who took the place of Moses as leader of the people? [Joshua:1:1-2].

4. What promises did the Lord make to Joshua? [Joshua:1:5].

5. Did the people obey Joshua? [Joshua:1:16-17].

The Christian's Thanksgiving

[Psalms:107:1-43].

Memory Verse: "Every good gift and every perfect gift is from above"

(JAMES 1:17).

～

Giving Thanks

God expects us to be thankful to Him for all His blessings. If we have thanks in our hearts we also have love. God wants us to love Him, for He loved us so much that he sent Jesus to die for us and take away our sins. How thankful we should be to Jesus for the awful suffering He went through for us! He did it to keep us from suffering. We should never forget to thank Him with all our hearts for His goodness and love.

Thanks unto the Lord

Sometimes we remember to thank our parents and our friends for kind things they do for us, but perhaps we forget that every good thing we have comes from God. Unless He gave them to us we should not have them. He gives us the sunshine and the rain, which makes things grow, and He gives us food. He gives us the air we breathe. He gives us health, or heals us if we are sick. He gives us parents to love and care for us. He gives us kind friends to be with us and help to make us happy.

The Best Gift

Most of all, and best of all, He gave us Jesus to take away our sins and to show us how to live so that we may make Heaven our Home forever and ever. Heaven is a beautiful place – no sickness there, no sorrow, no dying. Jesus tells us that He has gone to prepare a place for us, and where He is we may be with Him always.

Jesus takes good care of us while we are here on earth and love Him and do the things he tells us to do. We should always remember to thank Him.

Learning to Pray

A group of children who had never learned to pray were told by a teacher that they should talk to God as they would talk to a kind father. They should tell God what they wanted just as they would tell their own loving father. The children did that for two days. Then the teacher said that they would do it for one more day. But a little girl who had never learned to pray but had learned to say "Thank you" to her parents and others, said, "We asked God for something, and I think it would be nice to say 'Thank you' to God." That little girl was right; too often we forget to say, "Thank you, God, for all the things You give us." We should thank Him for Jesus, for His death on the Cross, for the Bible, for our church, for our Sunday School, for Christian parents, for His love, for His care of us, and for every other good thing He has given us.

Unthankfulness

In the Bible we read that one day as Jesus entered into a village, He was met by ten men who were sick with leprosy. When they saw Jesus, they asked Him to have mercy upon them. Jesus told them to go show themselves to the priests; and as they obeyed Jesus' command, they were healed. However, only one of the ten men came back to Jesus and fell down at His feet and thanked Him for this healing. Jesus then said, "Were there not ten cleansed? but where are the nine?" Wouldn't you think that all ten should have come back to thank Jesus?

From the East and from the West

We are to be thankful to God that He loves all people — people who live in the North, the South, the East, the West. The colour of their skin or the country from which they come makes no difference to God. He wants them to ask Him to forgive their sins and make them His children.

There is a beautiful picture of Jesus with children of many countries. He is holding one in His arms, but He loves them all. And Jesus wants to forgive their sins and have them live with Him in His Home in His beautiful Heaven.

God does everything just right, and we must never forget to thank Him, to love Him, and to do what He tell us to do.

Questions:

1. Does Jesus help people who are in trouble? [Psalms:107:13]; [Psalms:50:15].

2. Does Jesus want us to praise Him in Church? [Psalms:107:32].

3. Does God remember the poor? [Psalms:107:41].

4. How many daily blessings can you name which we receive from the Lord?

5. Does Jesus want us to be thankful for all things? [Ephesians:5:20].

Two Brave Spies

[Joshua:2:1-24].

Memory Verse: "Perfect love casteth out fear"

(I JOHN 4:18).

～

Going into the Land

The people were in a camp near the Jordan River. Joshua was getting them ready to go into the new home to which Moses and Joshua had been leading them. No doubt, they were very tired of wandering in a wilderness and not having a permanent place to stay. They were looking forward to the land where they could build their homes, dig wells for water, plant crops, feed their cattle, and build an altar and worship God. God had promised it to them.

Joshua Encouraged

God told Joshua that He would be with him as he had been with Moses. Joshua knew that it would not be an easy task to bring the people into that good land, but God told him to be brave and to trust Him to help them.

Joshua told the people to prepare their food, and be ready to cross the River Jordan. They did not have boats in which to cross the swift, broad, and deep river. But God knew what He would do to help them.

From across the river the people could see the high walls of the city they would have to take later on. Joshua said the women and the children should wait until it was safe for them to go. God always cares for those who need Him.

The Spies

Then Joshua sent two men to see what the country was like, what the dangers were, and what would be the best way to take it. But the king of the country had heard about the people while they were marching through the wilderness, and he was afraid of them. When he heard that some strange men had come into his country he went to look for them, and, perhaps, kill them.

They came to the house of a woman who was kind to them. She hid them under some stalks upstairs in her house. And when the king's men came to look for them they did not find them.

She told two spies that she believed God had given their people the land. She had heard how God had helped them, that He had even dried up the Red Sea so they could cross it. Evidently she believed in the true God instead of in idols.

The Thread in the Window

Then she asked them to be kind to her father and mother, to her brothers and sisters, and to her. The spies promised that in return for her kindness to them they would be kind to her and her family. But they told her what she should do. She should tie the "scarlet thread" -- perhaps a rope -- in the window of her house so that the soldiers would know which was her house and not destroy it. Her family should be sure to stay inside the house.

Then she let the two men down over the wall with the scarlet thread, or rope, and tied it in her window as the men had told her to do. When the soldiers came to take the city her house was not destroyed, because they saw the read thread in the window. It pays to be kind, and it pays to obey. God, no doubt, had told the men what to tell her; and when she did what they said, she was doing what God wanted her to do. People are always safe when they trust God.

Questions:

1. Had the people of Jericho heard about the Children of Israel? [Joshua:2:10].

2. Were the people of Jericho afraid? [Joshua:2:11].

3. How did Rahab make it possible for the two spies to escape? [Joshua:2:15].

4. Where should Rahab's whole family meet in order to be safe? [Joshua:2:18].

5. What kind of token did she put in the window? [Joshua:2:21].

ABOUT THE AUTHOR

Olukemi Akinrinola, MD is a wife, mother and a fulltime Pediatrician. She is popularly called Dr A by her patients and their family. The only daughter among seven children, she remembers racing for her father's daily newspapers and books as a toddler. She has been writing short novels since she was 11 years old. Dr A and her wonderful husband, Ola, are usually on the move with their 3 children; 2 boys and 1 girl. She loves singing and dancing with her 2 boys. Her daughter, on the other hand, loves to dance alone.

Dr Akinrinola's passion for imparting medical knowledge is evident in her roles as Clinical Professor of Pediatrics at the University of Dakota and at the Rocky Vista University in Parker, Colorado.

She and her husband are Associate pastors at their local church, Kingdom Connection Christian Center in Aurora, Colorado. They are also the founders of MIDASH ministry, a community outreach to Veterans and their passion is helping people reach their full potential.

www.ingramcontent.com/pod-product-compliance
Lightning Source LLC
Chambersburg PA
CBHW022113280326
41933CB00007B/373